OUR HEAVENLY FATHER

Activity Book

Faith and Life Series

BOOK ONE

Ignatius Press, San Francisco
Catholics United for the Faith, New Rochelle

Nihil Obstat: Rev. Msgr. Daniel V. Flynn, J.C.D.
                Censor Librorum
Imprimatur: + Joseph T. O'Keefe, D.D.
                Vicar General, New York

Director: Rev. Msgr. Eugene Kevane, Ph.D.
Assistant Director and General Editor: Patricia I. Puccetti, M.A.
Writer: Barbara M. Nacelewicz
Artists: Gary Hoff, David Previtali

Catholics United for the Faith, Inc., and Ignatius Press gratefully
acknowledge the guidance and assistance of Reverend Monsignor Eugene
Kevane, former Director of the Pontifical Catechetical Institute, Diocese of
Arlington, Virginia, in the production of this series. The series intends to
implement the authentic approach in Catholic catechesis given to the
Church in the recent documents of the Holy See and in particular the
Conference of Joseph Cardinal Ratzinger on "Sources and Transmission of
Faith".

Contents

1 God Is Our Father

Things to Do:

1. Take a walk outside and look at the trees, the clouds, and the sky that God has made. Now try to think of what the world would look like without these things. Say thank you to God your Father for these gifts.

2. Ask your family if you can say a prayer aloud before you eat dinner tonight. In your prayer, thank God for your food and your family.

Activity:

On the other side of this page circle the things God created. Underline the thing that man made. Then color the pictures.

Name: _____

2 *Heaven Is Our Home*

Things to Do:

1. Tell your family about your home in Heaven and how God wants all of you to come and live with Him someday. Tell them that you will all be very happy there for ever and ever.

2. Think of what for ever means.

> Think of how long a week is
> Then think of how long a month is
> Then think of how long a year is
> Then think of hundreds of years
> And then thousands of years.

Heaven is longer than that because it never ends. It is for ever!

Activity:

Write a letter to your heavenly Father on the next page.

Dear _Heavenly Father,_

(Tell your Heavenly Father how much you would like to <u>come</u> to Heaven.)

I would like to _Game to Heaven to see you._

(Now ask your Heavenly Father to help you get to Heaven.)

Please help me _to Love you and to obey you._

Love,

Grace

(Write your name here.)

8

3 *God Watches Over Everything*

Things to Do:

1. Try to imagine what it must have been like before God made anything. Remember, there was no world, no stars, no sun, no moon, and no outer space.

Then try to imagine God making the world, the sun, the moon, and the stars out of nothing.

2. In your book, can you find the words God used when He made everything?

Activity:

Angels do not have bodies and so we cannot see them. But we draw them to look like men in long robes with wings. Color the picture of the angel on the next page.

Name: _____

4 *God's Special Gifts*

Things to Do:

1. Use some of the gifts that God gave you:

    Look at a picture. What do you see?
    Listen. What do you hear?
    When you eat dinner tonight, what do you taste?
    Touch something. How does it feel?
    Go into a garden and sniff. What do you smell?

Say thank you to God for the gifts of your senses.

2. Talk to your guardian angel right now. Tell your angel if you are happy or sad. Now ask him to help you do what is right.

Activity:

Can you solve the puzzle ?

MY B _ _ _   +   MY S _ _ _

= _____

(Write your name.)

Here are some words to help you solve the puzzle:

SOUL   BODY

Name: _____

5 Adam and Eve

Things to Do:

1. Look in the *Words to Know* at the end of your book to see what the word "grace" means. Adam and Eve had grace in their souls when God made them. And you have grace in *your* soul.

2. Here is a play for you and a friend. One of you will be Adam. The other one will be Eve.

Adam: It's so nice here in the garden of Eden. We have everything we want.

Eve: And God is our good friend Who gave all this to us!

Adam: Even the lions and the bears are our friends.

Eve: It is so beautiful here. I'm very happy.

Adam: So am I, Eve. Let's thank God for His gifts.

Then Adam and Eve kneel down.

Adam and Eve: Thank You, dear Father, for creating us. And thank You for this beautiful place to live. *Amen.*

Activity:

Draw Adam and Eve in the Garden of Eden.

Put smiles on their faces because they were very happy in the garden. Then color your picture.

Name: _____

6 A Sad Story

Things to Do:

1. Think of one thing that you have done wrong. Tell God that you are sorry, and ask Him to forgive you.

2. When we sin, we say "No" to God. Plan how you can say "Yes" to God the next time you feel like doing something wrong.

Activity:

On the next page draw Adam and Eve in the Garden of Eden after they sinned. Make them sad because sin makes people unhappy. Don't forget to color your picture.

16   **Name:** _____

7 A
Time of Waiting

Things to Do:

1. In your book, can you find the names of two people who learned to love and obey God while they were waiting for the Savior to come?

2. Have you ever had to wait for something that you wanted very much? You think that the day will never come. But it always does. Imagine what the good people who were waiting for the Savior felt like.

Activity:

On the next page draw a picture of some of the animals that Noah is taking into the ark. Then color the picture.

18   **Name:** _____

8 *Getting Ready for the Savior*

Things to Do:

1. Imagine that you're Jesus' cousin, Saint John the Baptist, and you are getting people ready for Jesus to come. You would tell them to be sorry for what they have done that was wrong. You would tell them to love God and try to do what pleases Him.

2. Now *you* get ready for Jesus, the Savior, to come. Try hard to be very good and helpful before Christmas. Choose someone in your family to do something nice for each day. You might make the person's bed or make a card saying how much you love him or her.

Activity:

Can you find the missing words on the next page?

God gave Moses the

T_ _   C_ _ _ _ _ _ _ _ _ _.

The   P_ _ _ _ _ _   and

Saint John the   B_ _ _ _ _   helped

the people get ready for the coming of Jesus,

the Savior.

Here are the words to use in the puzzle:

PROPHETS   BAPTIST   TEN COMMANDMENTS

Name: _____

9 Mary Hears Some Wonderful News

Things to Do:

1. Next time you go to Church, remember to look at the statue of Mary. Mary is the Mother of Jesus. She was free from original sin from the first moment of her life. Ask her to help you love her Son, Jesus.

2. Here is a play for you and a friend. One of you will be Mary. The other one will be the angel Gabriel.

Mary is in her house all by herself. Then the angel Gabriel comes in.

Gabriel: Hail, Mary! You are full of grace. Among all women, you are most blessed. And blessed is the baby that you will have.

Mary: I don't understand. What do you mean? I'm afraid.

Gabriel: Don't be afraid, Mary. I'm an angel and God sent me from Heaven. He wants you to be the Mother of His Son.

Mary: I love God and so I'll do whatever He wants.
Gabriel: Thank you, Mary. Good bye.

Activity:

Draw Mary in her house and then draw Gabriel coming to tell her the wonderful news. Then color your picture.

Name: _____

10 *The Savior Is Born*

Things to Do:

1. Do you have a Christmas crib at home or at school? If you do, ask if you may set it up before Christmas. Only don't put the baby Jesus in yet. On Christmas Eve or Christmas morning, you can show that it is Jesus' birthday by putting Him in the manger.

2. Make Christmas cards for everyone in your family. Inside your cards write:

REJOICE AND BE GLAD

BECAUSE

IT IS JESUS' BIRTHDAY!

Then decorate your cards with a picture of the baby Jesus with Mary and Joseph. You can put the shepherds and angels in your picture too.

Name: _____

Activity:

Cut out Jesus and then paste Him in the manger.
Draw some straw and a blanket to keep him warm. And
then write THE SON OF GOD underneath the picture.
After that, color your picture.

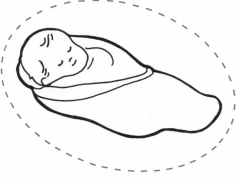

T _ _   S _ _   O _   G _ _

11 *Three Wise Men Arrive*

Things to Do:

1. Visit Jesus just like the wise men did. Ask your mother or father to take you to Church. Then ask them to show you where Jesus is in Church. You can go and talk to Jesus for a few minutes!

2. Christmas is Jesus' birthday. Since He is God, He doesn't need any presents, but your good deeds can be a real present for the Infant Jesus.

Activity:

Can you draw lines to match the blocks on this side. . .

. . . with the blocks on this side?

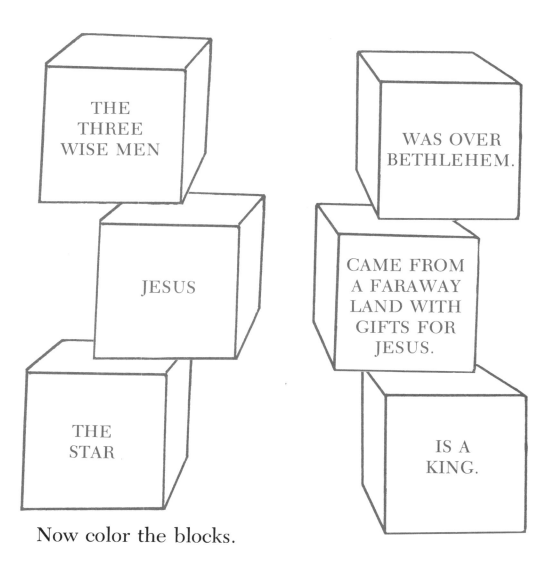

THE THREE WISE MEN

JESUS

THE STAR

WAS OVER BETHLEHEM.

CAME FROM A FARAWAY LAND WITH GIFTS FOR JESUS.

IS A KING.

Now color the blocks.

Name: _____

12 *Jesus Grows Up*

Things to Do:

1. Help your family with their work tonight just the way Jesus helped His mother, Mary, and His foster father, Joseph. You could set the table for dinner or help wash the dishes.

2. Can you tell how long ago it was that Jesus was your age? Ask someone to help you fill in the blanks below:

What year is this now?   —   — — — —

How old are you?   — — — —

Take away your age from the year.   — — — —

Jesus was your age that many years ago!

Activity:

Color the picture of Jesus' foster father, Joseph, working as a carpenter.

Saint Joseph, pray for us.

Name: _____

13 Jesus Begins His Work

Things to Do:

1. Look for some things in your house which remind you of Jesus. Is there a crucifix in your house? Is there a picture of Jesus?

2. Can you write in the names of the Twelve Apostles, who were Jesus' helpers?

M A T T _ _ _   T H O M _ _

P E T _ _   B A R T H _ _ _ _ _ _

J O _ _   T H A D D _ _ _

A N D _ _ _   P H I L _ _

J A M _ _   S I M _ _

J A M _ _   J U D _ _

Here are some words that will help you write the names:

SIMON THADDEUS PETER JOHN
JAMES JAMES MATTHEW ANDREW
JUDAS THOMAS BARTHOLOMEW PHILIP

Activity:

Draw a picture of Jesus and you together. Imagine that Jesus is telling you how much your Heavenly Father loves you.

Jesus gives _____ **an important message.**
(Write your name.)

14 Jesus Tells the Good News

Things to Do:

1. Find a copy of the Bible and look at it. It has the Good News of Jesus written in it. The priest reads from the Bible at Church. When you're older, you'll want to read it, too!

2. Do your parents read the newspaper at night? Make them a newspaper. Get a large sheet of paper and write

THE GOOD NEWS

at the top. Then write

GOD IS OUR FATHER

WHO LOVES US

VERY MUCH.

Put your newspaper with the one your parents read so that they can read them together.

Activity:

Draw a picture of yourself and someone that you love very much. Imagine that you are telling that person the Good News of Jesus.

_____ **tells** _____

     (Write your name.)   *(Write the name of the*
                                                      person you're telling.)

the Good News of Jesus.

15 Jesus Does Wonderful Things

Things to Do:

1. Here are some things for you to imagine:

Imagine that you are the one who has the five loaves of bread and two fishes. You take them to Jesus so that He can feed all the people who have been listening to Him. And he makes your loaves and fishes into enough food for everyone! What would you say to Jesus?

Imagine that you are one of the disciples and you are in a boat with Jesus. Then there is a terrible storm. You're afraid that you will fall into the water and be drowned. So you ask Jesus to help you. "Save us, Lord!" you cry. Jesus tells the sea, "Be still!" and everything is still. What would you say to Jesus?

2. Jesus would always help people who needed His help. He wants you to do the same. Are there people you know who are old or sick? If there are, can you think of a way to help them? Maybe you can visit with them or maybe you can make them pretty cards to help them feel better. Also, you can pray for them.

Activity:

You can make this get well card and take it to someone who is sick. Cut out the card and decorate it.

Name: _____

I hope that you are feeling better. I love you, and I am praying for you.

_____

Write your name on the line above.

16 We Believe in Jesus

Things to Do:

1. Tell Jesus that you believe in Him. Pray, "Jesus, I believe in You. Please help me to believe in You more and more."

2. Do you know someone who does not believe in Jesus? If you do, say a prayer that that person will believe in Jesus one day.

Activity:

At Mass, we use some of the same words that the man with the dying servant used when he asked Jesus to cure his servant. In the activity on the next page, draw a circle around the words that are the same. CLUE: Notice how some of the words are darker than the rest.

This is what the man with the dying servant said:

1. "Lord, I am not worthy for You to enter my house. But only say the word and my servant shall be healed."

And this is what we say at Mass before we go to Communion:

2. "Lord, I am not worthy to receive You. But only say the word and I shall be healed."

Name: _____

17 *The Best Gift of All*

Things to Do:

1. When you go to Mass this Sunday, watch for when the priest holds up the little round bread and the cup. It is just before this time that the bread and the wine in the cup becomes the Body and Blood of Jesus. Talk to Jesus. Say, "Jesus, I believe that you are there."

2. Watch the people going to Holy Communion. They are receiving Jesus. Next year, you may be able to receive Him, too.

Activity:

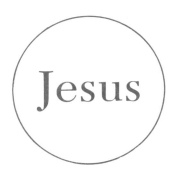

Jesus

This is the round, white bread (called a host) that the priest uses at Mass. When he says the special words, the bread becomes the Body of Jesus. Color it white.

Jesus

This is the cup (called a chalice) that the priest uses at Mass. It has wine in it and when the priest says the special words, the wine becomes the Blood of Jesus. Color it gold.

Name: _____

18 *Jesus Dies for Us*

Things to Do:

1. Remember to look at the pictures on the sides of the Church. These show the story of how Jesus was taken and nailed to a cross. These pictures are called the Stations of the Cross.

2. Ask someone at home to time you for three minutes. Sit quietly and think of the three hours that Jesus was hanging on the cross before He died. Then thank Jesus for dying to win back grace for you.

Activity:

Here are some pictures from the fourteen Stations of the Cross which you read about in your book. Read the story and then color the pictures.

Jesus had to carry a Cross through the streets of Jerusalem.

Mary suffered when she saw the way people were hurting her Son.

The soldiers nailed Jesus to the Cross at Calvary.

Mary and John stood by Jesus. After three hours Jesus died for us.

Name: _____

19 Jesus Was Raised to New Life

Things to Do:

1. Color some Easter eggs. Do you know why we color eggs at Easter? Because an egg is a sign of new earthly life, and Jesus died to give us new life with Him in Heaven.

2. If you get a basket of candy at Easter, share it with your family and friends. Easter is a happy day because Jesus rose from the dead, and you want others to be happy, too.

Activity:

The picture on the next page makes us think of Easter. Do you know why? Color it.

The egg is a sign of new life.
Jesus gives us new life.

46   Name: _____

20 *Jesus Begins the Church*

Things to Do:

1. Ask someone to show you the Pope the next time that person sees a picture of him or the next time he is on TV. The Pope is the leader of the Catholic Church.

Ask your parents who your bishop is. Ask them if they can show you a picture of him.

2. Say a prayer for the Pope and your bishop. Say, "Dear God, please help the Pope and my bishop to be good and holy leaders. *Amen.*"

Activity:

On the next page, draw yourself and your family going into a church for Mass on Sunday. Then color your picture.

48   **Name:** _____

21 *Jesus Goes Back to Heaven*

Things to Do:

1. Go outside and imagine that Jesus is there and He's just about to go back to Heaven. Imagine that He tells you that He will come back at the end of the world to take you to Heaven to be with Him for ever.

2. Look in your book for the promises that Jesus made before He went to Heaven. They are:

(1) Jesus promised the Apostles to be with them always even if they didn't <u>S</u> __ __ Him.

(2) Jesus promised to send the <u>H</u> __ __ __ <u>S</u> <u>P</u> __ __ __ __ to help them.

Activity:

Draw a picture of Jesus rising up into the sky and going back to Heaven. Then draw some of the apostles who are watching Jesus go. Don't forget to color your picture.

This is a picture of the Ascension.

Name: _____

22 *The Holy Spirit Comes*

Things to Do:

1. Ask your family if they will say this prayer with you: "Come to us, Holy Spirit, and fill our hearts with Your love."

2. Look in the *Words to Know* section of your text (page 117) and see who the Holy Spirit is. And do you know who the other two Persons of the Blessed Trinity are? Well, if you cannot remember, all you have to do is make the Sign of the Cross:

"In the name of the 1) _____,

and of the 2) _____,

and of the Holy Spirit. *Amen.*"

Activity:

Of course, we can't see the Holy Spirit because He doesn't have a body, but we sometimes draw Him to look like a dove, which is a kind of bird. Color the picture.

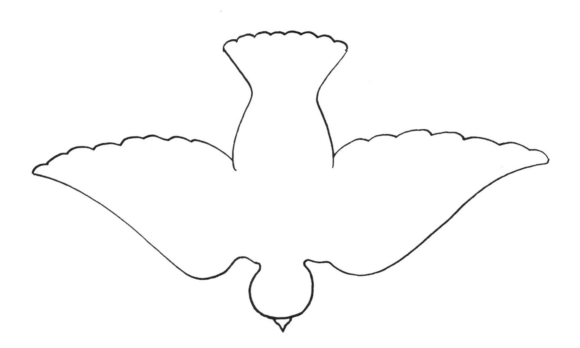

The Holy Spirit helps us to love one another and become holy.

Name: _____

23 *The Blessed Trinity*

Things to Do:

1. Make the Sign of the Cross. This reminds you of the Blessed Trinity:

"In the name of the Father, and of the Son, and of the Holy Spirit. Amen."

Activity:

There are three Persons but only one God. A shamrock helps us to remember. Look at the shamrock on the next page. There are three parts but only one shamrock. Write the names of the three Persons of the Blessed Trinity on the parts and then color the shamrock.

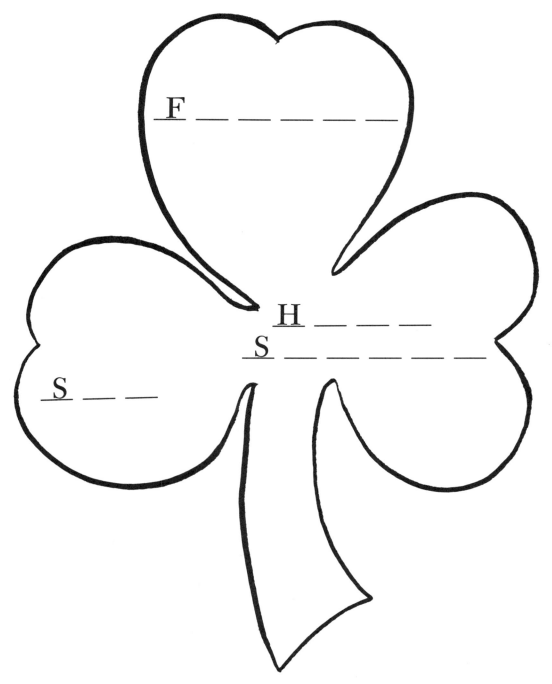

F _ _ _ _ _ _

H _ _ _

S _ _ _ _ _ _

S _ _

Here are the names of the three Persons of the Blessed Trinity:

FATHER   SON   HOLY SPIRIT

Name: _____

24 God Gives You His Life

Things to Do:

1. Ask your parents about your baptism. Here are some questions you can ask:

"Where is the church in which I was baptized?
What is it called?"

"Who are my godparents?"

"What did I wear?"

"Why did you give me the name you gave me?"

"How did the priest baptize me?"

"Was there a picture taken?"

"Did you have a party after my Baptism?"

Activity:

Can you find the missing words of the puzzle?

When I was born, I had the guilt of

O R _ _ _ _ _ _   S _ _ on my soul.

But then I was baptized and my soul was washed

clean and filled with the G R _ _ _ Jesus had

won for me. I became a member of God's family,

the C H _ _ _ _

Here are the words to help you solve the puzzle:

CHURCH   GRACE   ORIGINAL SIN

Name: _____

25 *Many Gifts From God*

Things to Do:

1. Take your textbook to Mass. Open to the part called *We Go to Mass*. (It is in the back of your book on page 113.) Try to follow what the priest and the people are doing.

2. When you get home try to remember as many things as you can about the Mass.

Activity:

Do the activity on the next page. On the first present write down three gifts that God has given you. Look at the second present to see how you can thank Him. Then color the presents.

God's gifts to me: **I thank God at Mass:**

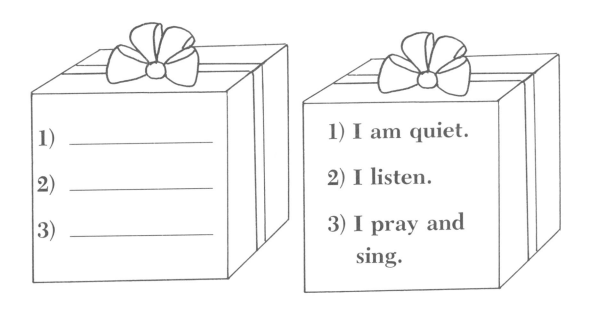

1) _____

2) _____

3) _____

1) I am quiet.

2) I listen.

3) I pray and sing.

CLUES:

Here are some gifts that you've received from God. You can choose three of these or maybe you can think of some other ones. On the lines above just write the part of the sentence that is darker:

> **God made me.**
> God has given me **my family**.
> God gives me **grace**.
> God gives me **food**.
> God has given me **my own angel**.

Name: _____

26 Our Mother, Mary

Things to Do:

1. Tell your mother and father about your other Mother in Heaven. Do you know her name? It is Mary.

2. Look for things in your house that remind you of Mary. Do you have a statue or medal of Mary? Do you have a Rosary?

Activity:

Mary has shown us a way to have peace on earth. Can you solve the puzzle to see what the way is?

Here are the words to help you solve the puzzle:

SACRIFICE   PRAY

Name: _____

27 Following Jesus

Things to Do:

1. Before you get into bed tonight, check off each thing as you do it:

☐ Kneel down by your bed.
☐ Make the Sign of the Cross.
☐ Thank God for everything that He has given you today.
☐ Tell Him that you are sorry if you have not been as good as you should have been today.
☐ Ask for His help to be good tomorrow.
☐ Ask Him to bless you and your family.

2. Tomorrow morning:

☐ Get out of bed.
☐ Kneel down by your bed.
☐ Make the Sign of the Cross.
☐ Offer God everything that you will do, think, and say today.
☐ Ask God to bless all the people you love and all people everywhere.

(Do these activities before doing the next one.)

Activity:

Follow the Leader: Here is a good way to follow Jesus. Cut out the footprints of Jesus, turn them upside down, and mix them up. Pick one each day and follow Jesus in the way that the footprint tells you to.

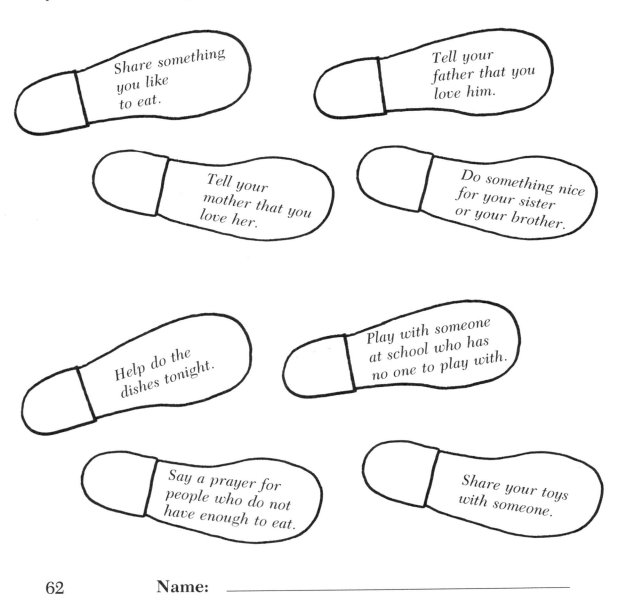

Share something you like to eat.

Tell your father that you love him.

Tell your mother that you love her.

Do something nice for your sister or your brother.

Help do the dishes tonight.

Play with someone at school who has no one to play with.

Say a prayer for people who do not have enough to eat.

Share your toys with someone.

Name: _____

28 Jesus Will Come Again

Things to Do:

1. Try to think of seeing Jesus in Heaven. What will be the first thing that you would like to say to Him? What will He say to you?

2. Think of seeing your Heavenly Mother, Mary. What will she look like? What do you think that she will say to you?

3. Think of seeing your grandparents, your parents, and your brothers and sisters in Heaven. None of them will be sick or tired or sad or worried. You will all be very, very happy.